By Laura Lyn

Copyright ©2010 by Laura Lyn.

All rights reserved

No part of this publication may be reproduced, stored in a retrieval system, or transmitted in any form or by any means electronic, mechanical, photocopying, recording or otherwise without the prior permission of the author.

The medical information in this book is not intended as a substitute for consulting your physician. All matters regarding your physical health should be supervised by a medical professional. The author or the publishers do not accept any responsibility for the application of any methods described in this book. The author believes this book should be available to the public for educational purposes.

Only those who receive accreditation through the Angel Ray Healing™ Certification course may teach the materials presented in this publication.

Table of Contents

FORWARD 1
DEDICATION 2
IN LOVING MEMORY 3
INTRODUCTION 4
PART ONE ANGELS HEALING RAYS 7

    CHAPTER ONE ARCHANGEL ZADKIEL 11
    CHAPTER TWO ARCHANGEL RAZIEL 18
    CHAPTER THREE ARCHANGEL MICHAEL 24
    CHAPTER FOUR ARCHANGEL RAPHAEL 31
    CHAPTER FIVE ARCHANGEL JOPHIEL 37
    CHAPTER SIX ARCHANGEL GABRIEL 43
    CHAPTER SEVEN ARCHANGEL URIEL 49
    CHAPTER EIGHT WHAT'S NEXT? 56

PART TWO - ANGEL ENCOUNTERS 58

    AN ENCOUNTER WITH AN EARTH ANGEL
    BY LAURA LYN 59
    MY ANGEL ENCOUNTER – WHY I DO WHAT I DO
    BY JENNY SMEDLY 62
    MY EXPERIENCE WITH ANGELS
    BY MANDY LORINCHACK 67
    MY ANGEL RAY HEALING EXPERIENCE
    BY JEANNE GRIMES 69

PART THREE - ANGEL MESSAGES 75

    ARCHANGEL CASSIEL AUGUST 12, 2009 77

ARCHANGEL JOPHIEL DECEMBER 25, 2009 78
ARCHANGEL CHAMUEL SEPTEMBER 9, 2009 79
ARCHANGEL ARIEL OCTOBER 23, 2009 80
ARCHANGEL URIEL SEPTEMBER 23, 2009 82
ARCHANGEL RAPHAEL AUGUST 20, 2009 83
SARIEL JULY 22, 2009 84
ARCHANGEL AURIEL MAY 7, 2009 85
ARCHANGEL ARIEL JANUARY 12, 2010 86

PART FOUR - CHARTS AND REFERENCES 88

CHART ONE - THE CROWN CHAKRA 89
CHART TWO - THIRD EYE CHAKRA 90
CHART THREE - THROAT CHAKRA 91
CHART FOUR - HEART CHAKRA 92
CHART FIVE - SOLAR PLEXUS CHAKRA 93
CHART SIX - SACRAL CHAKRA 94
CHART SEVEN - ROOT CHAKRA 95
CHART EIGHT - ANGEL RAY AND TONE CHART 96
CHART NINE - MAJOR CHAKRAS CHART 97
CHART TEN - CHAKRA LOCATIONS 98
CHART ELEVEN - CRYSTALS CHART 99

GLOSSARY 100

INDEX 104

SOURCES 108

Forward

Do you believe that an idea is so powerful that it can create its own consciousness? It is amazing when you wrap your mind around this concept. Everything you see, hear, feel, and touch is a sense. Your awareness of this sense opens your world to phenomenal potentials that can be tapped into by simply asking and believing.

I have witnessed and felt the powerful energetic essences of angels since I was five years old. Many incidents in my life have drawn me closer to recognizing these potent rays of light.

My concept of angels is a little different than what you may have read in other books. It has come to my realization through work with these beings that consciousness on focused organized direction manifested these beings. The consciousness of healing brought Raphael, the consciousness of clarity brought Jeremiel... God and the wisdom thereof manifested light reproduced by this consciousness of goodness and truth and the ultimate path of immense love, these are the Angels. These light beings work through energetic vibrations of colors and tones.

In this reference you will learn what has come to be enlightened by path work with the angels. It is my hope that you will receive a healing by these words. Love is always the answer.

Laura Lyn,   Owner of Angel Rays LLC   September 2009

Dedication

This book is dedicated to my friends from Merging Hearts and the Earth Angels that I have been blessed to know as clients. Every one of you are a gift in my life, you are family. Special thanks go to Colette, Henry and Linda Knapp, Becky, Katy, Heath, Maria, S.I.G.H.T. and to the Angel Rays Community for truly believing and encouraging me to move forward with my gifts. Thank you my dear friend Sherri Brake of Haunted Heartland Tours. Thank you Dale Jr. and Erik Lute for your love and wisdom in helping me accomplish this goal of sharing the Angel Rays.

Dale, I could not have finished this book without you. Love is always the answer. Twin flames united again.

Rassouli special thanks for your wonderful art and contribution for the cover. Your gifts with color and vibration are a source of awe and inspiration.

Jami Phillips, thank you for the cover photograph, you are so talented.

Dyan, Jenny, Jeanne and Mandy, you are all gifts to the world and also to me. Your stories bring wonderful light to this book. Thank you so much for your contribution.

In Loving Memory

Dear Papa,

You taught me about the angels and it was because of you I witnessed them throughout life. I know I am always protected with their rays of light and for this I am always grateful. I love you Papa.

Your loving Granddaughter,
Laura

Introduction

I was introduced to angels as a child by my doting Grandfather Leonard Pickens who I called Papa. He did this quite by accident, but I am sure there were divine intentions from the beings at play. My grandfather was worried that the noise and confusion from a fireworks display would create havoc in my over sensitive system. I seemed to jump at the smallest sound and run away or towards any spectacle or distraction in my path. I was a very hyperactive child and in my grandfathers wisdom he decided to tell me a story that I will always remember.

He shared with me his knowledge of angels, he said with every color and boom from the fireworks an angel was represented. The more colors and sounds the more angels. I remember sitting beside him as we tried keeping up with the fireworks by counting each one. We sat beside a small lake under a willow tree and in the waters reflective mirror I was counting more angels.

I was five years old during this angel's lesson. A few weeks after this experience I witnessed a glow in the corner of my room. I knew this glow was an angel. I had another vision and this time the vision took on tones and intense color. During this vision I was told my grandfather would have to go away. I was assured that I would always be protected even without my grandfathers' presence.

Three weeks later my grandfather passed away. From that time on I have been in the presence and communication with these light beings. My Grandfather helped open up my world to other realms that have led the way to wonderful explorations and insights.

I have waxed and waned in my spiritual path throughout my life. I have many experiences that some would perceive as a darker side. I am grateful and would not change any of my past life experiences. My shadow self has helped me learn to love people in all walks of life. If I would not have experienced the "darker side" I would not be who I am today.

Many gifted people walking on this earth are confused and depressed. I hope this book helps lessen the guilt, remorse, pain, and agony that some may be shackled to. With the gifts that I have, I have seen and witnessed many ugly facets of life. There was a time in my life when I had terrible depression and as a result I abused alcohol and substances. During these darker times I was shackled by fear. Ironically during these dark times I also received much insight and blessed healings.

People who have a natural tendency to feel energy may also have certain vulnerability. I have come to realize there are earth bound beings (deceased people) that can and will try to exploit any energy possible so they can feel alive. People who can sense energy have a light about them and this light can emanate as a beacon to these earth bounds.

Angels come with healing rays of light to help us move forward in life. I like to call these powerful healing rays of light "Angel Rays". The realizations that came upon me over the years have served me well to help people (both alive and deceased) find their light within. The angels assist us in becoming healthy mentally, physically, and spiritually so that we can help others do the same. It becomes a contagious and yet wonderful work when we can grab onto that light and move forward, becoming joyful beacons of light.

Let your light shine!

Part One

∞

Angels Healing Rays

Throughout sacred writings and the angelic lore, seven archangels have been represented as seven rays of color and these have been correlated to the seven master chakras. An angel is a messenger and an intermediate. It is my belief that everything is connected. The angel is the connection through the ultimate expression of love (God) to the intermediary (Ray of Light) to the individual expression of God (You).

These powerful Angel Rays are received frequently. You may receive the gifts of these rays by prayer or positive thought processes. Angels are more than happy to share their light. The angels can assist all of us in being healthy spiritually, physically, and mentally.

This collection of enlightened knowledge comes from both mediumship (the act of receiving messages from another realm) and from my extensive research and experience with angels. I am combining what I have learned from my council (guides, teachers, masters and angels) with what I have learned in books from the order of angels.

When working with the Angel Rays you are enacting their frequency of light to help illuminate and clear your chakra. This work can profoundly enable you to move forward if you decide to accept the freedom. When the attunement of the ray is received, I believe a cleansing takes place deep in the cellular tissue of the physical body and in the auratic field (the energy field around the body).

Each Angel Ray Attunement per chakra has a different frequency. By allowing the different frequencies in our field we are receiving divine light from an ultimate force that understands our needs in a way that transcends time. This means we are not only receiving healing for ourselves but also for our ancestry root. I believe everyone holds deep ancestral memory in all their cells. When we connect to these frequencies we are accepting healing in a profound way. This in turn helps replace fragmented structures that can now be sealed and healed.

It has been interesting to watch people who have opened themselves to the Angel Ray Healings. I have witnessed people release years of agony, phobias, heartache, and habits. You can open up to allow the Angel Rays to heal you. Simply ask and believe.

Each chapter will outline the Angel Ray and the chakra involved. The type of healing energy you are seeking will depend on your individual situation. The chapters will clearly outline the angels, chakras, intent of use, colors, and tones associated thereof. The outline will also include situations where each attunement may be helpful. You can enact one, two or all if you wish during a session. You can do this in the privacy of your own home. It is my hope that you learn and feel comfortable enough to try this on your own and feel the energies that pour forward upon activation.

These incredible rays of light have always been there for our use. The angels are delighted to be utilized to help us on our journey. They celebrate an opportunity to work with us. They all have abundant rays and are more than eager to share and express their ultimate power of energy.

I consider angels to be higher consciousness of love. Each angel comes with their own energy source. Just as the sun has an energy source that radiates its light upon the earth as rays, so do the angels when requested.

When reading the upcoming chapters it may be helpful to listen to soft flowing music in the background. Angel's frequency of light is enhanced by tones and notes. The song playing on the front page of my website www.angelreader.net can be useful for this. The music hits all the notes that work though the chakras.

Each Chapter has several pages to take notes. Have a pen or pencil ready so you may write down any insights that come through while reading. You may be surprised at how much of your own knowingness and higher self is activated by simply reading these words. Allow the energy to pour forward because in doing so you are helping heal yourself.

It may feel different working from the Crown Chakra to the Root Chakra; this is how the angels and my guides instructed me to teach. If you feel more comfortable beginning with the root, that is fine, go with what feels natural for you. In Part Four - Charts and References, you will find a diagram on chakra locations.

I recommend you read all the chapters first before starting the exercises. Once you have read all the content of part one you may work with any rays that apply to your needs.

Enjoy the information and allow it to be a guide for your future work. Ask the angels for a deep healing and enlightened pathway that will guide you through your individual path. Ask the angels to bring inspiration to further clarify and define your mission. They are there to help if you simply ask.

Chapter One
Archangel Zadkiel

Violet Ray
Crown Chakra

Archangel Zadkiel is a powerful angel who manifests deeply with those who know their higher self. When I encounter Zadkiel I am aware of his unconditional love and above all comfort. He is the angel of mercy, and is known as "the holy one" who teaches one to have faith and trust in God.

Zadkiel will help bring forth blessings of abundance in many different ways. Opportunities will be displayed in your life to open to a deeper truth. His teachings are of the ways of tolerance. Deep joy comes forth when attuning to his energy, so call upon him when experiencing self doubt or insecurities. This will inspire the truth that you are one with God and one with blissful joy.

Zadkiel will bring a calming attribute when going through chaotic or turbulent experiences. He is the rescue remedy source through God that can help you know and realize the truth that you are not disconnected. When facing addictive traits you may call upon Archangel Zadkiel to help remove blocks and fears so you can release and restore to the state of being whole and natural.

With his attribution towards the brain mechanism through the pineal gland, he will assist with the immune functions throughout the body. Zadkiel also governs the higher organs and glands associated with the brain. He is wonderful to call upon when feeling down or under the weather.

Zadkiel is a best friend to most mystics, psychics, and alchemists through sacred geometry. He inspires the imagination and frees one to explore higher potentials. The heightened vibrations that he works through inspire open beings to explore the truths of total connectedness. He enables you to be the visionary.

Zadkiel is associated with the Crown Chakra. When aligned, this chakra is powerful beyond expression. You are truly liberated and hold the power to move beyond limitations commonly granted by untruths of shackles and fears. This will activate your sight for visions, quests, love, and light. This will empower you to serve mankind and spirit alike. Determination and imagination will set you free. Soaring into the cosmos is a blissful adventure.

You may burn a violet candle when attuning the Crown Chakra with Zadkiel. Placing your name into the wax along with the name Zadkiel will further amplify this process.

Ways to bring in Zadkiel's Violet Ray and boost your crown chakra energy:

- Focusing on dreams and writing down one's visions and intentions. Quiet contemplation, meditation and yoga. Listening to guided meditation tapes. Taking spiritual courses.

- Vibrational tones of the note B and Chanting (EEE).

- Use aromatherapy oils such as Lavender, Jasmine, or Magnolia.

- Wear or carry a violet gemstone. Violet stones would be amethyst crystal, iolite, purple quartz, and purple jade.

Meditative Statement

Hold the appropriate crystal in your non dominant hand. Raise your dominant hand in the air, breathe deeply and when in your mind's eye you perceive the color violet allow it to pour into your hand. Move your hand onto the top of your head and crown chakra area. Breathe deeply and appreciate the radiating effect of the ray by acknowledging and giving thanks. Again breathe deeply and read the following statement:

Archangel Zadkiel,

I give you thanks and honor for helping me become attuned to your Violet Ray of light. I thank you for basking me with this energy that will enable truth and joy to guide me. I ask that this Violet Ray of light heals and restores me to my natural state of perfection. I accept that your ray will help bring me to a new level that will manifest restorative energy. That for the greatest good, I accept your Violet Ray into my Crown Chakra.

Archangel Zadkiel Message

Dearest Ones,

I come to you hoping you will see and hear the patterns of life. Look around and you will see eloquent symbols everywhere that will show you deeper truths. Everything is connected, the seed goes into the earth, the earth nourishes the seed, the seed explodes, and the seed becomes a trunk, leaves, limbs, branches and roots. This is true with everything. Every fiber of life is synergistically intertwined.

I ask for you to open your eyes wide. See all the gifts being presented throughout the day to help you on your travels and journey. I am here to help you find your inner truths that will set you free. Your seeds are your ideas; allow them to explode in wondrous ways.

Blessings and Love,
Archangel Zadkiel

Chapter One – Archangel Zadkiel

Notes from Archangel Zadkiel

Chapter One – Archangel Zadkiel

Notes from Archangel Zadkiel

Chapter Two
Archangel Raziel

Indigo Ray
Third Eye Chakra

Archangel Raziel's name means "Secret of the Creator" and holds keys to sacred mysteries. Raziel holds the universal secrets and personifies divine wisdom. He is the holder of originality and human expression of insight. He comes through in pure ideas through your dream world. When seeking clarity he is always there to help lighten the veils. The encounter with Raziel may feel intense. Once the energy is activated, life will never be the same. Raziel awakens prophets and religious reformers, this power should be used lovingly and wisely.

While you are in meditation Raziel will bring a charged essence. He helps you find yourself through focus and understanding. When thought patterns become obsessive he can bring great ease. I have chosen Raziel many times when my son who is a true indigo child becomes overly excitable. I have also found Raziel to be extremely helpful during times of anxiety and confusion.

Raziel is a wonderful help when feeling physical pain. He will help release negativity when sought. Insomnia can become a thing of the past when evoking his ray of light for this condition.

The Third Eye Chakra is associated with intuition, clairvoyance (seeing), clairaudience (hearing), and clairsentience (sensing). The Third Eye acts as a window to that which is mostly unseen within the typical senses. When activating the Third Eye you are inviting latent psychic senses to open and truths to be revealed. Information flows from Raziel divinely. Wisdom from the ages comes forth while opening and attuning to this marvelous ray of light.

You may burn a dark blue candle when attuning the Third Eye with Raziel. Placing your name into the wax along with the name Raziel will further amplify this process. You may strengthen the energy by holding in your non dominant hand a Celestine crystal.

Ways to bring in Raziel's Indigo Ray and boost your Third Eye Chakra energy:

- Star gazing, meditation.

- Use aromatherapy oils such as Patchouli, Frankincense, and Myrrh.

- Music such as Mozart or Bach. Chanting (AYE) and Vibrational tones of the note A.

- Wear or carry an indigo gemstone or silver jewelry. Indigo stones are Celestine, Tourmaline, and Tanzanite.

Meditative Statement

Hold the appropriate crystal in your non dominant hand. Raise your dominant hand in the air. Breathe deeply, and when in your mind's eye you perceive the color indigo, allow it to pour into your hand. Move your hand onto your brow area where your third eye lays. Breathe deeply and appreciate the radiating effect of the ray by acknowledging and giving thanks. Again breathe deeply and read the following statement.

Archangel Raziel,

I give you thanks and honor for helping me become attuned to your Indigo Ray of light. I thank you for basking me with this energy that will enable clarity and wisdom to guide me. I ask that this Indigo Ray of light opens and guides me to my natural state of perfection. I accept that your ray will help bring me to a new level that will manifest insight and awareness.

That for the greatest good, I accept your Indigo Ray into my Third Eye Chakra.

Archangel Raziel Message

I come to you with the intent to help you open up to realms of explorative inspiration. I am present to help you realign with your true nature of spirit. As you allow our energies to emerge into your auratic field, you will open to powerful truths that will change your earthen self forever. As you ask the openness will begin. All the hosts of the highest realms are fully supporting your evolution and growth at the pace that is best for your vibration. Everything is in perfect order, every experience and lesson is truth that holds keys for your imprinted energy.

Blessings and Love,
Archangel Raziel

Notes from Archangel Raziel

Notes from Archangel Raziel

Chapter Three
Archangel Michael

Blue Ray
Throat Chakra

Archangel Michael focuses a healing Blue Ray of light for your throat chakra. The throat chakra is the energy center located in the neck. The throat chakra focuses energy through speech, writing, and your creative processes. When you deprive your truth because of fears, your throat chakra tightens and or becomes less capable of moving energy to the right spin. Prior uncomfortable experiences (in this body or past lives) of being ridiculed or not validated for speaking can also close or slow this energy center.

The Blue Ray represents authority and power. Never be afraid of your truth. By allowing Archangel's Blue Ray toward and into your throat chakra you are claiming empowerment in your ideas, words, and beliefs. It is good to bring your truth forward in the form of speech.

When being attuned to this Blue Ray of light you will notice a new intuitiveness coming upon you. You will be able to feel people's energy in a new and profound way. When people are sad, confused, shy, or even angered you will be able to feel their energy and have an opportunity to help them in the form of prayer.

A new sense of clarity in speech will prevail. Eloquence of speech patterns seem to shape rapidly after attuning to Archangel Michael's Blue Ray. The throat and its processes (larynx, thyroid, and esophagus) all benefit from Archangel Michael's Blue Ray.

You may see yourself speaking in front of a group of people with a new confidence. Anxiety levels may diminish. The distractive habit of rerunning argumentative conversations (what I could have said…) will cease to be part of your thought patterns.

Archangel Michael is so interesting to work with. He has a mighty protective light that is ready to shield when asked. He is the commander of his "legions of light" (angels that focus light on mankind). I suggest that everyone ask Archangel Michael to bring protection with his intense strength.

When you attune the throat chakra with Michael, light a blue candle. Place your name into the wax along with the name Michael to further amplify this process. You may strengthen the energy by holding a Labradorite crystal in your non dominant hand.

Ways to bring in Michael's Blue Ray and boost your throat chakra energy:

- Poetry, art appreciation, meaningful conversations. Taking self-development courses. Attending spiritual functions.

- Journaling. Neck and shoulder rolls.

- Use aromatherapy oils such as Patchouli, Geranium, Chamomile, Peppermint, Mint, and Cypress.

- Music that is repetitive, such as echoes or sounds of ocean waves (Michael has a roaring vibration) Vibrational tones of the note G and Chanting (EYE).

- Wear or carry a blue gemstone. Blue stones would be Labradorite, Lapis Lazuli, Sapphire, and Blue Agate.

Meditative Statement

Hold the appropriate crystal in your non dominant hand. Raise your dominant hand in the air. Breathe deeply, and when in your mind's eye you perceive the color blue allow it to pour into your hand. Move your hand onto your throat area. Breathe deeply and appreciate the radiating effect of the ray by acknowledging and giving thanks. Again breathe deeply and read the following statement.

Chapter Three – Archangel Michael

Archangel Michael,

I give you thanks and honor for helping me become attuned to your Blue Ray of light. I thank you for basking me with this energy that will enable protection and strength. I ask that this Blue Ray of light heals and restores me to my natural state of perfection. I accept that your ray will help bring me to a new level that will enable open communication with self and all.

That for the greatest good, I accept your Blue Ray into my Throat Chakra.

Message from Archangel Michael

Dearest Ones,

Every experience you have lived through has brought you to a place of self-resilience. Focusing on your highest intentions will ensure you are going on your pathway to discover your deepest truths. Each soul must work through hurt and pain in order to grow and move beyond the past. No person can take this pain from another. Despair always surfaces when the old and new are clashing. You are on the verge of a new, higher vibrating stage of life. This transformation will bring new ideas and heightened thinking will manifest. A new space and identity is evident for those who choose this direction.

Chapter Three – Archangel Michael

Allow me to help you assimilate the new energies in your earthly realm. When you are able to fully confront and deal with the lower vibration emotions, you'll be ready to absorb the higher vibrations. Ask for my cloak of protection to cover you while releasing toxicities and receiving the highest light and honor the endless flow of new direction and order. This order will bring restorative peace, happiness, and expressional love.

Allow your heart to reach for this new gift of life!

Blessing to you and yours always,
Archangel Michael

Notes from Archangel Michael

Notes from Archangel Michael

Chapter Four
Archangel Raphael

Green Ray
Heart Chakra

I can spot a healer across the room when I see the Green Ray of Raphael shooting around the unsuspecting holder. When I am facing an individual and see the Green Ray, it is emerald in color and has a certain gleam that envelops the sitter. I enjoy meeting healers; it brings happiness when I see that a healer has heard their call and took on a mission to help others (people or animals).

I teach that Raphael can be evoked and amplified by burning green candles and asking for a deep healing. Chisel the name of the person to receive healing energies from Raphael into the candle.

Raphael is one of my greatest friends. He has helped me throughout the years in so many ways. I have seen true miracles in play with my clients when working with him. Try to work with him often, health is so important and he is eager to assist.

What's most important to activate Raphael into action is honesty. Do you really want to receive the healing? Could there be hidden turmoil deep within the cellular pattern that is prohibiting you from receiving a healing? In order for this or any other healing to work, deep truth is always needed. We all create obstacles; sometimes, these are merely lessons. Be mercifully honest with yourself and divine healing will transpire.

On a physical level you will begin seeing changes in pain tolerance. Tension headaches will be far less painful/frequent. The emotional response will be noticed by less tension and anxiety. Mental confusion will fade away and a new alertness will be received. Your emotional well being will take on a new level.

Spiritual essence will spark by your ability to visualize becoming a healer for yourself and others. The act of merely thinking good healthy thoughts will amplify and multiply Raphael's Green Ray. You may strengthen the healing energy by holding an aventurine crystal in your non dominant hand. Aventurine is one of my favorite stones, it helps create abundance.

Ways to bring in Raphael's Green Ray and boost your Heart chakra energy:

- Nature hikes, spending time with family or friends, surrounding yourself with plants, gardening, taking self-love courses, reading romantic novels or watching romantic movies, candlelight dinners.

- Use aromatherapy oils such as Eucalyptus, Pine, Tea Tree, Cedar wood.

- Music that has the sounds of nature. Vibrational tones of the note F and Chanting (AH).

- Wear or carry a green gemstone. Green stones would be Aventurine, Emerald, Jade, Malachite, Peridot.

Meditative Statement

Hold the appropriate crystal in your non dominant hand. Raise your dominant hand in the air. Breathe deeply, and when in your mind's eye you perceive the color green allow it to pour into your hand. Move your hand over your heart area where your Heart Chakra lays. Breathe deeply and appreciate the radiating effect of the ray by acknowledging and giving thanks. Again breathe deeply and read the following statement.

Archangel Raphael,

I give you thanks and honor for helping me become attuned to your Green Ray of light. I thank you for basking me with this healing energy that will enable me to become healthy. I ask that this green Ray of light heals and restores me to my natural state of perfection. I accept that your ray will help bring me to a new level and that it will bring enhanced energy and harmony.

That for the greatest good, I accept your Green Ray into my Heart Chakra.

Message from Archangel Raphael

Dear Ones,

I come to you with intent to help you release any negative patterns that have caused you to slow your process of growth. I am working on a cellular level, repairing tissues, and purifying your bloodstream to remove toxins that have been trapped deep within the cell walls as forms of emotions. I love you unconditionally and will help you open your heart center. Your true essence and higher self will shine by accepting my healing ray.

With Love Dear Ones,

Raphael

Notes from Archangel Raphael

/ Chapter Four – Archangel Raphael

Notes from Archangel Raphael

Chapter Five
Archangel Jophiel

Yellow Ray
Solar Plexus Chakra

When channeling messages for artists, writers, and extremely creative people, I most often see Jophiel. The ray of light and the healing aspect that he aligns to is the color yellow. Another name for Jophiel's Yellow Ray is the Sunshine Ray.

Jophiel is a good choice when wisdom is needed to help others. He helps release self doubt. Most Mediums (whether they are aware or not) are greatly influenced by his messages. Jophiel is one of the most accessible angels to tap into. When you are beginning to learn the art of mediumship I highly recommend working with him.

Jophiel works within the Solar Plexus and when attuned, a deeper doorway of wisdom will be revealed. He can help you achieve a higher understanding. He can also help you in recovery of soul fragmentation, if shattered by deep shock or abuse.

On the physical level Archangel Jophiel attunes to the pancreas, liver, spleen and stomach. When there is sluggishness, rejuvenation happens with his essence. He can help remove toxins and plaques from the cell walls.

Mental awareness and enhanced astuteness will be felt after your attunement with Jophiel. You will find laughter coming easily. Self esteem issues will diminish. Communication will be improved because of the creative essence that is activated.

Spiritually you will feel a stronger connection to angels and enlightened beings. You will have an enhanced ability to connect to your higher self and seek knowledge thereof.

You can further amplify the Yellow Ray by holding a piece of Amber or Citrine in your non dominant hand. Jophiel can also be amplified by burning a yellow candle. Chisel by pencil, pen, or a toothpick the name Jophiel into the candle.

Ways to bring in Jophiel's Yellow Ray and boost your Solar Plexus chakra energy:

- Taking classes, creative photography, reading informative books, doing mind puzzles. Developing one's memory.

- Use aromatherapy oils such as Rosemary, Lemon, Grapefruit, and Bergamot.

- Music that is mentally stimulating such as chimes. Reed and Horn Instruments. Vibrational tones of the note E and Chanting (OH).

- Wear or carry a yellow gemstone or something gold. Yellow stones would be Citrine, Amber, and Topaz.

Meditative Statement

Hold the appropriate crystal in your non dominant hand. Raise your dominant hand in the air. Breathe deeply, and when in your mind's eye you perceive the color yellow allow it to pour into your hand. Move your hand above your navel where your Solar Plexus lays. Breathe deeply and appreciate the radiating effect of the ray by acknowledging and giving thanks. Again breathe deeply and read the following statement.

Archangel Jophiel,

I give you thanks and honor for helping me become attuned to your Yellow Ray of light. I thank you for basking me with this energy that will enable creativity and balance to guide me. I ask that this Yellow Ray of light heals and restores me to my natural state of perfection. I accept that your ray will help bring me to a new level that will manifest restorative energy.

That for the greatest good, I accept your Yellow Ray into my Solar Plexus.

Archangel Jophiel's Message

Dear Ones,

Today is the day to wake up and feel the beauty that nature exhibits! Feel the frequencies that nature offers. Allow the colors to embrace you with every breath. As you align yourself to what the mother has to offer, I will help open up those places deep within your mind's eye that will create a new consciousness of splendor and profound creativity. You will soon feel yourself alive with this power of life. Allow yourself the truth of your inner wealth and knowledge. Open to this seed and you will activate your drive to generate your own inner art.

With love and honor Dear Ones,
Archangel Jophiel

Notes from Archangel Jophiel

Notes from Archangel Jophiel

Chapter Six
Archangel Gabriel

Orange Ray
Sacral Chakra

Archangel Gabriel will help restore balance and clarity in your life. He helps people find their inner strength. He will help reveal your life plan. I have worked with this angel extensively to help many people release their patterns of depression. Working with Gabriel will bring deep joy and fulfillment.

The Orange Ray transmits to the kidneys and adrenals. When the adrenals are in good order a heightened energy response becomes accessible. This brings forth a new vitality and balances other systems networking with hormones.

Releasing grief is another response to expect after this attunement. Self respect, joy, and positive social interaction will be easier to achieve. You may find your creative spark and a new positive approach to life after activating the Orange Ray.

You will notice an elevated intuitive response, greater focus, enthusiasm and a powerful revelation of "life is good in this spiritual body" will personify. If you want it, you have it! The answer to life is expecting joy and energy through awareness, and truly believing that it can be achieved. It takes courage to accept these gifts.

Gabriel's energy can be amplified by burning an orange candle. Chisel by pencil, pen, or a toothpick the name Gabriel into the candle. You can further amplify the Orange Ray by holding a piece of orange calcite in your non dominant hand.

Ways to bring in Gabriel's Orange Ray and boost your sacral chakra energy:

- Aromatic baths, water aerobics, deep tissue massage, emotional movies, cooking classes, embracing sensations (such as different food tastes).

- Use aromatherapy oils such as Melissa, Orange, Mandarin, and Tangerine.

- Vibrational tones of the note D and Chanting (OOO). Harp, meditative music with deep resonating patterns, or music that flows (running water, thunderstorms, etc.).

- Wear or carry an orange gemstone or copper piece. Orange stones would be Orange Calcite, Coral or Carnelian.

Meditative Statement

Hold the appropriate crystal in your non dominant hand. Raise your dominant hand in the air. Breathe deeply, and when in your mind's eye you perceive the color orange allow it to pour into your hand. Move your hand onto your lower navel area where your Sacral Chakra lays. Breathe deeply and appreciate the radiating effect of the ray by acknowledging and giving thanks. Again breathe deeply and read the following statement.

Archangel Gabriel,

I give you thanks and honor for helping me become attuned to your Orange Ray of light. I thank you for basking me with this energy that will enable me to focus and move forward. I ask that this Orange Ray of light heals and restores me to my natural state of perfection. I accept that your ray will help bring me to a new level that will bring restorative energy.

That for the greatest good, I accept your Orange Ray into my Sacral Chakra.

Archangel Gabriel's Message

Dear Ones,

I am here to remind you that within your spear, the childlike joy and wonder that you were born with is still alive and well! We want for you to attain your greatest joys and to have a heart so fulfilled that it bubbles over. We will open up the universe and all its answers, all you need to do is ask. We delight in bringing new ideas, explorations and truths. We are never hidden away for only the Gurus of the Nations exposure. We are here present for you Dear Ones! Ask and you shall receive the great news! Open up for these great truths and allow them to excite your inner being. As they become clear you will have a quickened state of being. Jump with joy and radiate your smile forward!

We love and honor you Dear Ones
Archangel Gabriel

Notes from Archangel Gabriel

Chapter Six – Archangel Gabriel

Notes from Archangel Gabriel

Chapter Seven
Archangel Uriel

Red Ray
Root Chakra

It has been my experience that whenever a person needs to be more grounded Uriel is needed. Uriel has a powerful grounding effect. Call on Uriel when you are confused, tired, dismayed or even overzealous and airy.

Uriel's ray influences the root chakra. His role is to help you evolve and grow. As the tree starts with just a seed, each idea is a seed, for this seed to manifest and bud it needs nourishment to sustain and thrive. Uriel will help provide this nourishment through insight and empowerment.

Uriel will bring his ray through the base of your spine when directed to do so. Ask Uriel to shine his light and share his beam of energy so you can focus on your endeavors in a more organized manner. He will bring in more focus if you are studying for exams or readying yourself for a new career.

When you need direction Uriel's light will help you move forward with each step.

The energy associated with past traumas of physical or emotional abuse can dissipate by allowing his ray to flow within. This will help alleviate other symptoms which may seem to have no connection with a particular condition (phantom pains).

Physically Uriel's Ray will focus on reproductive organs, your circulatory system, detoxifying blood, lower trunk area, knees, legs and lower back.

Emotionally Uriel's ray will approach primal arousal of lust and desire. His essence will help release energy that has been blocked deep in tissues. This will bring courage and resiliency.

His ray helps us identify and align to our purpose in life. It helps us be in that spiritual conscious connection to the supreme order. This will help bring physical energy, stability, willpower, and security.

It is helpful to light a red candle while evoking his energy. By writing his name into the wax prior to lighting the candle you are amplifying your intent for his work. You are acknowledging his fire energy and appreciating his gifts. By holding a piece of Hematite in your non dominant hand to the base of the spine you can further amplify and orient his healing ray.

Ways to bring in Uriel's Red Ray and boost your Root chakra energy:

- Incorporate physical activities such as an exercise program or yoga.

- Use aromatherapy oils such as Sandalwood, Ylang Ylang or Juniper.

- Stimulating music with deep beats such as drums or music that makes your body move like Latin American music. Also use vibrational tones of the note C and Chanting (UH).

- Wear or carry a red gemstone. Red stones would be Red Tiger's Eye, Garnet, Red Jasper or Ruby.

Meditative Statement

Hold the appropriate crystal in your non dominant hand. Raise your dominant hand in the air. Breathe deeply, and when in your mind's eye you perceive the color red allow it to pour into your hand. Move your hand onto the base of your spine where your Root Chakra lays. Breathe deeply and appreciate the radiating effect of the ray by acknowledging and giving thanks. Again breathe deeply and read the following statement.

Chapter Seven – Archangel Uriel

Archangel Uriel,

I give you thanks and honor for helping me become rooted and attuned to your red ray of light. I thank you for basking me with this energy that will enable me to focus and move forward. I ask that this ray of light heals and restores me to my natural state of perfection. I accept that your ray will help me with my mission here on earth.

That for the greatest good, I accept your red ray into my Root Chakra.

Archangel Uriel Message

Dear Ones,

It is time to prepare for your deep transformation and ascension. You are reconnecting with the creator but the truth is you were never unconnected. Your feelings of being disconnected were an illusion. The reality is that you (as all) are connected with everyone and everything. Remember who you are, live, love and order within your own unique energy. Finding your power in this energy will help you transform and grow into the powerful light being that you already are. Focus on this inner light and allow it to transmute and multiply. When you embrace the idea of deep joyous living you are already multiplying this light. Walk with me and you will know a new focus, a profound truth will be your every step. You are beauty and love.

Hold on and multiply your light loved one.
Archangel Uriel

Notes from Archangel Uriel

Notes from Archangel Uriel

Chapter Eight

∞

What's Next?

Now that you have read through all the Angel Ray chapters it's time to decide how you want to use this knowledge. As mentioned at the beginning of the book you can evoke the powerful energies in prescribed order, or you may work in the order that suits yourself comfortably. If you have one chakra that you would like attuned by an Angel Ray this would be appropriate and correct. The point is to trust your own self in knowing what is needed in order to move forward. All you need to do is believe and accept the vibrational healing.

When I am giving Angel Ray Healings I am channeling messages from the angels and guides asking for their assistance. Usually more than one angel comes forth for an individual. This book introduced seven angels that are focused in each chakra.

The crystals, vibrational music and angels work synergistically to synchronize perfect harmony within your body. This energy is always available to enhance balance.

You can activate the healing effects as many times as you would like. I recommend three full Angel Ray Healing sessions to my clients.

I am currently giving Angel Ray Healings™ at my office. I am seeking individuals who would like to become Angel Ray Practitioners™. If you are interested in certification please contact me at Laura@angelrayhealing.com.

Part Two

∞

Angel Encounters
Celestial and Earthen

Several friends sent in contributions to help highlight their individual stories about angels. I have a personal belief that we also can encounter angelic energies here on earth through people. I call these people Earth Angels. Please enjoy the stories about Earth and Celestial Angels. While reading you may have memories of your own that will help you realize you too had an angelic encounter.

An Encounter with an Earth Angel
by Laura Lyn

I have always been attracted to fanciful colors and waves in art. There are certain artists who seem to have a keen pathway to heightened vibrational energy. This is a story about a friend that I met and the experience I gratefully received while basking in his art.

When I was a child I encountered my angel's rays of light entering from the right corner of my bedroom wall. This started my fascination with colors and rays. For hours I would watch the shimmering light through the draperies. I would fixate on the streams of light coming from branches and leaves through the swaying trees. I felt there was wondrous energy in the lighted rays. As a young child I felt this energy explode as the angel showed her essence. I could somehow feel the energies in the rays of natural light.

As I grew I became interested in colors and would paint for hours upon hours. I would try to replicate the vision that I saw when I was five years old. I was unable to control where the paint went or the application of the colors. The flow on the canvas always seemed different than what I perceived in my mind's eye. Frustration mounted and I finally gave up, I would not be an artist.

Back in 2003 my friend helped me by designing a website. She found some artwork for me that she felt would suit it nicely. I was mesmerized when she unveiled the site and all its artistic flow. I was excited and quickly asked, "Who's the Artist? How did you get permission?" She shrugged and said "I don't know, don't worry, there are a million sites, he won't ever know..." I was livid. Determined to find the artist, I poured over websites daily.

After several unsuccessful years I decided to put a web video together featuring his artworks with the caption "Help Me Find This Artist". This did not work but the universal energy at play (power of intention) did step up and here is what happened.

In February 2009, my boyfriend decided to surprise me by making one of my dreams come true. He designed a set of Oracle Cards with pictures of the artwork from my website. It was a great surprise. I was so excited to hold in my hands these wonderful healing pieces of art. I was enchanted and proclaimed that we needed to find this artist.

About an hour later I heard a loud yell "LAURA!!!" I ran into the office afraid that he had been shocked or hurt. "Laura, I found him!!! I was confused and asked "who?" He explained "Rassouli Laura, I found Rassouli the artist!"

We found a phone number on his site so I excitedly called and left a message about how long I had been looking for him. He called me on the following day which was my birthday. I felt like I had known him for years. He was warm and gracious. I explained I had a deck of cards that I wanted him to see and asked if he lived near Los Angeles where I would be visiting the next week. As it turned out he lived within a few miles of where I would be visiting. A week later I was welcomed by Rassouli to his studio. He greeted me with a grand hug. I felt like I had known him for many lifetimes. He ushered me in and suggested that I enjoy the studio while he painted. I almost passed out by being overcome with emotion. I cried while watching him magically express his higher knowingness on the large mural canvas. Waves of angelic energies flew around the room. I was brought back to when I was five and I broke down and cried. I was so over whelmed with joy that I could hardly contain myself.

In my eyes, Rassouli is the finest Fusion Artist on the planet. The healing energy nested in his canvas is undeniable. When you look at one of his works you are embracing energies of the Goddess and Angels alike. Please go to www.rassouli.com and experience for yourself why I love Rassouli so much. Drop him a line and let him know how much you appreciate the healing touch he so generously gives.

The cover of this book was gifted by my wonderful friend Rassouli, whom I will always be grateful for meeting.

Part Two – Angel Encounters

My Angel Encounter
Why I Do What I Do
by Jenny Smedley

I started to get a two way connection with 'somebody up there' the very first time I appeared on TV. It was Belfast - and it was a late night chat show - Kelly. I had never been on TV before in my life, and I was terrified. I wasn't a good flyer, so I was already unsettled by the flight when I got there, and I knew that Belfast audiences were renowned for being tough, and I was going to be talking about reincarnation. I was going to be on 'live', with the show going out as we made it, so there was no room for error.

I was shown into the 'green room' and told I was to be the last guest, 'top of the bill' as it were - which only added to my terror. The green room at UTV overlooks the studio area and the producer pointed out the floodlit chair down below, saying "You'll be sitting there." I was starting to think that I'd have to make a bolt for it. A live audience, a live performance and a subject, which, while dear to me, was a well-known foil for comedy! What on earth was I doing there? I went through the procedure; make-up, wardrobe, and then I found myself standing in the wings, looking across the cable-strewn floor of the set. I could see the audience members peering over the scenery to see who was coming on next. I can honestly say that if my publisher wasn't standing right behind me, blocking my escape route, I would have done a runner right then and there. I looked across at the 'hot seat' I was about to occupy, and knew for a certainty that I was going to freeze. No way could I walk across that gap.

I heard the commercial break announced and received a nudge from behind. The very next thing I knew, I was sitting, surrounded by giant cameras, the audience a menacing blur behind them, facing a total stranger across a desk - Kelly. I had no recollection of propelling myself there. The commercial break ended, the questions began, and the answers....just came, from nowhere.

Later that year I was travelling to Norwich from Somerset, on a train, to take part in a Christian based programme called Sunday Morning. Given that I'd done several TV shows by then talking about my past life experience, I knew enough to be aware that this was going to be a tricky one. I was asking myself what the purpose of all this was - wise enough by now to know that making a living from book sales (hopefully) wasn't any kind of reason for being! I was with a friend and I told her that I wanted some quiet time to meditate. I knew that I was being put 'up against' a regular presenter on the show - a vicar's wife, who was going to argue that reincarnation would never be accepted by Christianity, and so I knew I was going to need some help.

I went into one of the deepest trances I'd ever experienced. I could literally feel my vibration increasing, leaving the train far behind in another reality. I could still hear the sound of the train in a peripheral sort of way, but it really didn't exist in the same plane as me, and if it had suddenly caught fire I could well have been impervious to the knowledge.

All of a sudden I found myself in a "presence". At the time I had no idea what it was. I had an impression of vast golden light towering above me. I had an overwhelming tidal surge wash over me – a love so deep, that it transcended human love by a magnitude. This love was given and reciprocated on an equal footing. It's very hard to describe the whole gamut of emotion and feelings that flooded through me. It can only be understood when it's experienced. It is overwhelming, and makes it very clear in a second, that all we know and hold dear of this physical world is as unimportant in reality as a grain of dust in the vastness of the Universe. The feeling was almost like a dog and master, it terms of devotion, but with absolutely NO subservience at all. The love and the obligation was given and received in total equality. I felt divine, and yet at the same time I was like a child wanting to please a parent. Not because I felt I had to or out of duty, but because pleasing the parent would fill me with joy and double my own happiness.

I was shown a scenario by this being; it contained three paths; one central path and two smaller ones running parallel with it. The side paths were my first book, and my connection to a past life soul mate. The central path showed a person (who could have been me) being given the role of 'seed planter'. This person would set seeds in people, while sharing her story with millions all over America. I was shown that this person would be attacked at times, maybe even physically, and might eventually have to live in a protected environment. The 'being' paused, while I considered what I was patently being offered.

Instinctively, without any hesitation at all, I said, 'Let me! Let me!' I was desperate and determined to be given the task of seed planter. I would have done whatever I had been asked. Making this being happy was the very same thing that would make me happy. The being said, "OK" – just that. It was simple, but it was binding. I only found out later that I had 'made a contract with an angel'.

Needless to say, when it came to the interview, the answers, as always, were there. I was placed firmly on my pathway, and I've been on it ever since. Every time things seem to slow down, a new tool emerges, and off I go again! Like I said, knowing why you're here and walking with purpose in the direction you know unshakably is right, is essential to well-being.

www.jennysmedley.com

Jenny Smedley Based in beautiful Somerset, in the UK, DPLT is a past life therapist, an author, TV and radio presenter/guest, international columnist, **angel consultant**, and the UK's leading expert in the subject of **past lives**.

Angels have been a huge part of Jenny's life, ever since a life-changing angel visitation. She considers herself very lucky to have been put onto her life path by this angel, and has been given gifts (such as the ability to create unique, personal angel portraits), in order to help her achieve her role in this life.

My Experience with Angels
by Mandy Lorinchack

I have had many experiences with angels. I will share with you a couple that stick out the most in my mind. The first one was when I was about 17 years old. I was driving to my boyfriend's house and it began to snow. Soon I was trying to drive in white out conditions up a hill towards an overpass. I soon lost control of my car and was spinning out of control. It was almost like I was moving in slow motion, though oddly, I wasn't scared. When my car finally came to a stop, I was able to kick my door open in the deep snow. I got out and realized I had come just inches from going over the bridge. I wasn't quite sure what I was going to do. I was alone on a secluded road, at night, and at a time before cell phones. So I decided to start walking and noticed a jeep coming towards me. The jeep stopped and a man got out. I never really saw his face and he didn't speak to me, he just smiled and helped me get my car out of the ditch. When my car was back on the road, I got out to thank him and realized he was gone. No tire tracks in the snow, no cars on the road, just gone. That's when I realized I had just been saved by my guardian angel. I felt overwhelmed with gratitude.

The second one that I remember most happened when my husband and I were in the process of buying our first home. Anyone who has ever bought a house knows how stressful the whole process is. I just remember waking up in the early morning hours and seeing this green glowing mist at the foot of our bed. It was so beautiful all I could do was stare. I felt just this awesome sense of serenity looking at it and in that moment I knew everything was going to work out.

I see bright flashing lights and glowing mists all the time. I am always fascinated by them and I always wish that I knew what they were trying to tell me. The colors are always just the brightest and most vivid shades I have ever seen. There really are no words that I could use to do them the justice they deserve. I just love seeing them. I see them everywhere... in my home, at work, at the store... everywhere. They're all different colors, and with each color usually comes a different emotion. Love, hope, determination, peace and comfort just to name a few, but always a positive feeling. With each one, no matter what emotion it carries, I always feel comfort. I am never scared...ever. My favorite one so far is the indigo... but I see all colors. Mostly yellow, green, blue, pink, purple and even white. I haven't figured out how to communicate yet, but I do know I feel incredibly blessed to have them around me and that I am able to see them. I make it a habit to thank them each day for everything they do for me and my family. My suggestion for everyone reading this book is to do exactly that. Thank your angels for protecting you and helping you. They are by your side always, watching over you, whether you see them or not.

Mandy is a friend and client of Laura Lyn who graciously shared her story. Thank you so much Mandy for your gifts!

My Angel Ray Healing Experience
by Jeanne Grimes

Laura Lyn has been my friend for nearly two years now. I feel blessed to be a part of her life. She has informed me through her wonderful Angel readings and has shared her unconditional love and guidance with me. As President of The Merging Hearts Holistic Center in North Canton, OH, I have included Laura Lyn in our organization's schedule for many angel meditations and enlightening workshops, such as her Realm to Realm sessions. She has provided us with numerous fund-raisers and has become an integral part of our organization's growth and well-being. We are truly fortunate to have her as a trusted friend and spiritual guide.

In addition to the Angel Readings and workshops, Laura Lyn offers healing sessions called Angel Ray Healings. They are offered as a set of three meetings and I have done two of them so far. During these sessions, you lay on a massage table in a darkened room. She has Incense and candles burning and there is wonderful angelic music filling the air. Laura Lyn starts the session with a prayer of protection and calls forth all the energies that will be for your highest good. She places stones and crystals at various points along your body, having standards for each of the chakra locations, but also listens to her guides for specific guidance as to what your body needs. She then calls in the various angels and their Healing Rays of Light to help heal your physical, emotional and psychological bodies. Archangels Michael, Uriel, and Gabriel are invited into the room to shed their healing Rays of Light upon you. Other angels and spirit guides enter the room as well to lend their healing power to the session. Laura Lyn continues to pray for guidance and healing and offers sincere gratitude to all those present. She may chant, sing, praise – whatever spirit moves her to do.

My first Angel Ray Healing session was profoundly soothing. I felt both energized and calm. I was refreshed and a little light-headed. It was a beautiful experience and the effects lasted for several days after the session. But my most profound experience happened during my second session with her.

During my second visit, I was again laying on the table enjoying the lilting music and fragrant scents that filled the room. Laura had placed the sacred stones at their critical points along my body and I was relaxing as her soft voice enveloped me with her love. As Laura continued calling in the angels with their healing rays of light, I suddenly felt myself sit up. I could feel something lift out of me. My spirit-self sat up. With my eyes closed, I could see in my mind's eye the back, the arms and the back of the head of this being. I felt a little startled and thought, "What's going on?" And then this being turned and looked over her left shoulder. She continued to rotate her body and left arm around and eventually turned her head around enough to look me in the eyes! She continued to gaze softly into my eyes and then she smiled. She smiled this gentle, knowing smile, much like the smile of the Mona Lisa. "This is who you are!" she said to me telepathically. Her eyes were almond shaped and beautiful and expressed an unconditional love and an ancient wisdom that was strong and knowing. Her body was in the shape of a human form, but she was glowing! She glowed with a white and golden light. She was luminescent! She literally glowed from within! If you've ever seen the movie Cocoon, there is a scene where the young female from another star system takes off her human skin and emerges as a glowing entity. That's what I really looked like! Absolutely stunning!

She (I) possessed a wonderful combination of strength and gentleness – a perfect balance of masculine and feminine energies. She knew all, loved all and was there to be of service to others. She possessed an inner strength and assuredness that was solid and steady, and yet a softness and quietness that radiated warmth and contentment.

As I continued to look into her eyes, I became aware of several other entities around us. They were glowing forms also but I couldn't see their faces. It looked as though they were wearing glowing capes that made them appear soft and willowy. I heard a voice that spoke for the whole group. It said, "You are one of us. You were the one from our soul group who chose to come here to Earth. We are proud of the work you are doing. We are here to assist you in any way.

We are here to help you, but you must ask for our assistance. We love you and want to help you on this journey."

And then they all faded away.

I'm still in awe of what I saw and heard during my Angel Ray Healing session. I've told many people about this vision because I think it's important for all of us to know two things. One, that we are all beings of light and love. We all glow from within and have an inner wisdom that is there for us to tap into at any time. We are balanced entities, whole and complete. We have strength from our masculine energies – an inner strength that comes from an inner knowing of Truth. And we are soft. We have a gentleness from our feminine energies that allows us to be compassionate and loving, warm and caring.

And secondly, we all need to recognize that we are not alone. We each have a soul group, a spiritual family, which watches over us and surrounds us with love and protection. This is our true family. We are the ones who are "away." They care deeply about our happiness and progress and are available to assist us. They want to help us in our endeavors but we must first ask for their assistance. They can not intrude and cannot assist unless asked. In the quiet times of meditation and reflection, ask your spirit family, or soul group, for guidance. Ask for assistance. Your spiritual family is here with you, waiting for your requests.

I've tried to use this experience to help me grow spiritually. I often visualize glowing bodies inside each person I see. It truly changes the way you look at people. For those we see who are angry or lost, they've truly forgotten who they are. For others, there is a glimmer of understanding inside. Sometimes your eyes will meet with someone who is seeing you as a glowing spiritual being. Your eyes communicate a knowingness of who you really are. There's such joy and love in those moments. I also try to envision my own glowing form inside this physical body. I imagine my luminescent body looking out through radiant eyes at the world, at the people and at the beauties of nature. When I look through those glowing eyes, instead of my thinking, analyzing eyes, the world looks softer and gentler. I feel like I've been reborn and look through new eyes. If only I could do this all the time. I forget. I forget who I really am. Even with having this wonderful, outrageous experience, I still forget who I really am. And then I breathe. And then I slow down. And then I remember who I truly am. And then I remember who you truly are, a spiritual being. A glowing form wrapped in a skin of earthly matter.

Remember who you are – a luminescent spiritual being who has taken a trip to Earth to learn and grow and help others on their journey here. Wake up to the Truth of our true nature.

Part Two – Angel Encounters

Merging Hearts Holistic Center
5590 Lauby Road, Suite 3B
North Canton, OH, 44720
http://www.merginghearts.org

Thank you my friend Jeanne for your insight and love.

You are sharing gifts with so many, we are grateful.

Part Three

∞

Angel Messages

Here you may enjoy more messages that I have channeled. When reading the messages please have soft music playing in the background. Musical tones help bring the angelic rays forward. This will help you receive the message in a very personal and profound way.

Try bringing forth your own messages from the angels by playing soft music, taking a deep breath, asking for the angelic message and start typing. You will be surprised what happens when writing. The magical words will spill forward almost effortlessly after a little practice.

Another way to receive personal messages is to clear your mind. Have a tape recorder ready and ask out loud for an angel to bring a message forward directly channeled through you. When you begin to talk don't worry if your words go in all different directions. You will eventually begin to articulate the beautiful passages from the angels without effort.

Before doing this either through speaking or writing, ask Archangel Michael to bring his protective light to you so you can receive the messages from the light beings. Have a white candle burning to help amplify the protective white light.

Part Three – Angel Messages

Enjoy the messages the angels brought me to share, and especially enjoy the messages that you receive personally from the angels of light.

Archangel Cassiel Message
Channeled August 12, 2009

Dear Ones,

Do not be afraid to release old ideas. What is harbored deep within the cells is trapping you, it is like a rusty anchor chained to the ship's mast that must be released to set free.

I am here to remind you that the past errors were lessons and they are not to be carried throughout life. You are harboring guilt and pain that no longer fits into your lightened being. Light and dark is very important. Remember the pain and then release it. Now capture onto the promise of a new day where joy and happiness presides.

Capture this light and you will capture the deep truth of love. We will never interfere but we will assist when being called upon to do so. It is your willingness that brings the healing into action. Be willing Dear one to open yourself to the idea of perfect health and perfect order. I will bring my healing light to you when you are ready to truly release the past.

Archangel Cassiel

Part Three – Angel Messages

Archangel Jophiel Message
Channeled December 25, 2009

Dear Ones,

The holiday season is so busy with the bustling and lively energies flowing every which way. Take some time to breathe in with gratitude all the love that surrounds you. Take a moment to get out in the cool fresh air to breathe in gratitude. Ask the winds to bring the confirmation onto you that you are love and loved so much from your higher energy sources and bring this deep gratitude to those around you.

The higher energy forces that work magically in your realm will move forward to touch all those in your beautiful circle to bring great blessings.

We are here to help you on your path of brightness and love. We welcome the opportunity to bring messages of love, comfort and joy onto you. We are always by your side gently whispering our heavenly guided inspirations so you can be your greatest self. Hear our words in the winds.

Dear One. You are love, light and beauty.

Blessings and beauty during this lovely season of Yule,
Archangel Jophiel

Archangel Chamuel Message
Channeled September 9, 2009

Dear Ones,

Welcome to the start of a new world! This world is the one we have been excitingly anticipating for a millennium. This is the life of feeling love and love becoming rampantly contagious! Welcome to the World Child and all it has to offer.

You are in control, you have the beauty and light deep within your cells that are ready to radiate out towards the highest of points. Feel this frequency as it moves! You may be aware lately that your ears are vibrating and a high pitch sound may be shimmering through. This is your brainwaves orientating you to your new higher frequency. With this new vibration you will have a quicker response to your higher knowingness. You will feel embraced with love. The love you will feel, there will be no words to explain in the English language. Trust and move forward with this new frequency, we will walk beside you as you get accustomed to the higher energies and ideas.

We welcome you.
Archangel Chamuel

Archangel Ariel Message
Channeled October 23, 2009

Dearest Ones,

Whenever doors close unexpectedly and life seems daunting remember there is a grand plan. We are always right beside you in your hour of need. We never forget your hurt, worry, loneliness or wariness. We are right beside you supporting your every step.

Patience and acceptance is a challenge that every human must partake. There are grand lessons in the air and when a human is up for the challenge we will be there ready to assist you in learning the lessons.

Remember back when a door closed in the past, it may have been a painful experience. Now remember what happened after the closed door, did you really lose? You most likely found a new strength and new sense of empowerment to move forward.

Trust in yourself enough to know the answers will always be revealed. We will work in the background to help set up opportunities that will help you shine. You are the answer! Believe and the answers will always come by believing in your own strength and by accepting help from those all around you in your hour of need.

Breathe, be aware of the light and love all around you, be grateful for the new opportunities coming your way.

We love you fully and completely,
Archangel Ariel

Archangel Uriel Message
September 23, 2009

Dearest Ones,

We are anxious and ready to bring the good news of joy, love, peace and surrender to you. We have been anticipating our communication with you and are gleeful at the opportunity to share our essence and frequency of truth.

Our objective is to help you receive a quickened state of joyfulness. A higher place within your cells, receiving this great joy will help you release decades and lifetimes of fear. Communicate with us frequently and we will help restore you to your natural spirited selves.

You are spirit; you carry upon you on the earthen level a sense of shackled pain, the truth is that is all an illusion. Bringing yourself back to your natural spirit, you will realize joy like you have never witnessed.

Hold onto this truth Dear Child and you will soar with the eagles even in your earthen now reality.

We look forward to soaring with you.
Archangel Uriel

Archangel Raphael Message
August 20, 2009

Dear Ones,

Identify and call upon me to heal you on all levels of your life, spiritually, emotionally, and physically. Feel my energy pulse through every cell in your body and cleanse it with my healing emerald light. Let go of the fear, dread, confusion...hold on to the love...release and renew every cell with my emerald ray of light.

As you heal remember who you are, an instrument of peace. You have abilities to see and hear truth! Hold onto that truth that you were born with! Your light is shining; it just takes a little belief to set it free to the world to share and express.

I am here ready to assist, simply ask.
Archangel Raphael

Sariel Message
Channeled July 22, 2009

Dear Ones,

You are in a great time of evolutionary transference. We are here to help enable you to the newness within every particle that is now beginning to illuminate. With every shift may come chaos.

You can purge the chaos by simply remembering this is based on fear. Fear not for this is the day that has been written in the records for true light to shine.

We walk beside you in a silent way. You can merge with us by simply believing and consciously stepping with us, open for truth. Truth is that you are love, you are light, you are whole, complete and new. Embrace this newness and hold on to the shiny ray of love.

Be in beauty, Dear Ones, with every step.
Sariel

Archangel Auriel Message
Channeled May 7, 2009

To you Dear Children,

Keep your hearts and minds open for this is where truth comes through. Your openness is essential for the pathway of peace is through your innocence and grace. Children, you are the chosen ones to bring the peace back to the world. You have a certain charge that will bring true growth and perfection for the future of the earth.

You hold the answers that will bring the kingdom of all the elements back to their intended nature. Your inspiration is key to saving your grounds and waters. Know you are the honored ones and the ancients will speak their truths to you. These truths have long been forgotten but you young ones will soon be able to retrieve and restore what has once been.

Archangel Auriel

Note: This message, meant for young ones and young at heart, brought with it a glow and warmth that stayed with me for over an hour after channeled. The glow was light pink, you may want to light a pink candle to help bring openness and restoration in. Please enjoy the essence and love that Archangel Auriel offers.

Archangel Ariel Message
Channeled January 12, 2010

Dear Ones,

Every day is an opportunity to explore and be part of the wonders that God has to offer. We love you unconditionally, we bring you messages, and we celebrate in your achievements. Always remember you are not alone, we are here to witness your growth. Hold your head high and know deep within that you hold the keys to the joyous life you are meant to live.

Strangers pass by and sometimes you see their pain. Project to them your love and graciousness. You are giving them an answer they can someday retrieve. You are the mirror of God! When you feel that conscious connection to the supreme holiness within your cells you are awakened to truth! You hold the universe right within yourself! You are connected to all and all is connected to you! Rejoice and feel the spirit that is embracing you with ultimate love and devotion. There is no reason to ever fear. Laughter, joy, happiness, these are the expressions towards life we celebrate for you.

Blessings and love,
Archangel Ariel

I hope you have enjoyed the angel's channeled messages. Please sign up for my monthly newsletter at angelreader.net to receive more messages from the angels. I would be delighted to help you individually learn how you can also channel messages from your angels. Please contact me so we can and have time for your personal message. Here you will learn who is coming forth through angelic frequencies.

Part Four

∞

Charts and References

This section contains the following easy to reference charts for further study:

Chart One - Crown Chakra	89
Chart Two - Third Eye Chakra	90
Chart Three - Throat Chakra	91
Chart Four - Heart Chakra	92
Chart Five - Solar Plexus Chakra	93
Chart Six - Sacral Chakra	94
Chart Seven - Root Chakra	95
Chart Eight - Angel Ray and Tone Chart	96
Chart Nine - Major Chakras Chart	97
Chart Ten Chakra Locations	98
Chart Eleven Crystals Chart	99

Part Four – Charts and References

Chart one

The Crown Chakra

Color	Violet
Sanskrit Name	Sahasrara
Location	Top of head
Lesson	Learning about one's spirituality. Our connection to the concept of "God" or a higher intelligence. Integrating one's consciousness and sub consciousness into the super consciousness.
Imbalances	Addictive traits, fears, immune problems, feeling disconnected.
Crown Stimulants	Focusing on dreams. Writing down one's visions and inventions. Violet gemstones and violet clothing. Using violet oils such as lavender or jasmine essential oils.

Chart Two

Third Eye Chakra

Color	Indigo
Sanskrit Name	Anja
Location	Forehead, in between the eyes.
Lesson	Intuition–The right to "see." Trusting one's intuition and insights. Developing one's psychic abilities. Self-realization. Releasing hidden and repressed negative thoughts
Imbalances	Learning disabilities, co-ordination problems, sleep disorders, insomnia, and physical pain.
Third Eye Stimulants	Star gazing. Meditation. Indigo gemstones and indigo clothing. Using indigo oils such as patchouli or frankincense essential oils.

Chart Three

Throat Chakra

Color	Blue
Sanskrit Name	Visuddha
Location	Throat region
Lesson	Relationships-The right to speak. Learning to express oneself and one's beliefs (truthful expression). Ability to trust. Loyalty. Organization and planning.
Imbalances	Thyroid imbalances, swollen glands. Infections. Mouth, jaw, tongue, neck and shoulders problems. Shyness, anger
Throat Stimulants	Singing (in the shower), poetry, stamp or art collecting. Meaningful conversations. Blue gemstones and blue clothing. Using blue oils such as chamomile or geranium essential oils.

Chart Four

Heart Chakra

Color	Green
Sanskrit Name	Anahata
Location	Center of chest
Lesson	Relationships–The right to love. Love, forgiveness, compassion. Ability to have self-control. Acceptance of oneself, anxiety, confusion.
Imbalances	Heart and breathing disorders. Chest pain. Tension. Passivity. Immune system problems. Muscular tension.
Heart Stimulants	Nature walks, time spent with family or friends. Green gemstones and green clothing. Using green oils such as eucalyptus or pine essential oils.

Chart Five

Solar Plexus Chakra

Color	Yellow
Sanskrit Name	Manipura
Location	Above the navel, stomach area
Lesson	Personal power–The right to think. Balance of intellect, self-confidence and ego power. Ability to have self-control and humor.
Imbalances	Digestive problems, ulcers, diabetes, constipation. Nervousness, toxicity, poor memory, low self esteem.
Solar Plexus Stimulants	Taking classes, reading informative books, doing mind puzzles. Sunshine. Detoxification programs. Yellow gemstones and yellow clothing. Using yellow oils such as lemon or rosemary essential oils.

Part Four – Charts and References

Chart Six

Sacral Chakra

Color	Orange
Sanskrit Name	Svadisthana
Location	Below navel, lower abdomen
Lesson	Feelings—The right to feel. Connected to our sensing abilities and issues related to feelings. Ability to be social and intimacy issues.
Imbalances	Eating disorders. Alcohol and drug abuse. Depression. Low back pain. Asthma or allergies
Sacral Stimulants	Hot aromatic baths, water aerobics, massage. Embracing sensation (such as different food tastes). Orange gemstones and orange clothing. Using orange oils such as 94elissa or orange essential oils.

Part Four – Charts and References

Chart Seven

Root Chakra

Color	Red
Sanskrit Name	Muladhara
Location	Base of spine, coccyx
Lesson	Survival-The right to exist. Deals with tasks related to the material and physical world. Ability to stand up for oneself and security issues.
Imbalances	Anemia, fatigue, lower back pain, depression. Frequent colds or cold hands and cold feet.
Root Stimulants	Physical exercise and restful sleeps, gardening, pottery and clay. Red gemstones, red clothing, bathing in red, etc. Using red oils such as ylang ylang or sandalwood essential oils.

Chart Eight

Angel Ray Tone Chart

Chakra	Archangel	Ray	Tone	Purpose	Crystal
Crown	Zadkiel	Violet	B	Focus	Amethyst
Third Eye	Raziel	Indigo	A	Inspiration	Celestine
Throat	Michael	Blue	G	Communication	Labradorite
Heart	Raphael	Green	F	Harmony	Aventurine
Solar Plexus	Jophiel	Yellow	E	Wisdom	Citrine or Amber
Sacral	Gabriel	Orange	D	Creativity and balance	Orange Calcite
Root	Uriel	Red	C	Devotion Grounding	Hematite

Part Four – Charts and References

Chart Nine
Major Chakras Chart

Chakra	Location	Function
Crown	Crown of the head	Knowingness and Higher Spiritual Information
Third Eye	Through center of forehead	Clear seeing and Clairvoyance
Throat	Base of neck and throat	Communication and Expression
Heart	Center of chest	Love, Ability to Validate and Be at Peace
Solar Plexus	Solar Plexus	Energy, Distribution and Personal Power
Sacral	Below the navel	Emotionality, Sexuality and Clairsentience
Root	Base of Spine	Survival in the Body and Security

Part Four – Charts and References

Chart Ten
Chakra Locations Diagram

Chakra	Color	Angel
Crown	Violet	Zadkiel
Third Eye	Indigo	Raziel
Throat	Blue	Michael
Heart	Green	Raphael
Solar Plexus	Yellow	Jophiel
Sacral	Orange	Gabrial
Root	Red	Uriel

Part Four – Charts and References

Chart Eleven
Crystals Chart

Crystal	Color	Purpose
Amethyst	Violet	Focus, harmony, healing and psychic development, Crown Chakra
Celestine	Indigo	Inspiration, enhances spiritual growth and awakening, Third Eye Chakra
Labradorite	Blue	Communication, it raises consciousness and connects one with universal energies. Very useful to deflect unwanted energy, Throat Chakra
Aventurine	Green	Harmonizing, peace and tranquility to hear messages, Heart Chakra
Citrine	Yellow	Restorative, excellent for times of chaos, stress, or self doubt, powerful stone for depression, Solar Plexus
Amber	Yellow	The wisdom stone, **Amber** absorbs negative energies and transforms them into positive, Solar Plexus
Orange Calcite	Orange	Creativity and balance, wonderful stone to help you feel at home and safe, Sacral Chakra
Hematite	Red	Devotion, grounding, feeling of unsettledness, Root Chakra

Glossary

Anja
Knowledge. Belongs to the chakra which is located between the eyebrows. Referred to as the third eye or brow chakra.

Anahata
Untouched. The chakra localized in the heart. Known as the heart chakra.

Angel Rays
Angel Rays are light frequencies that are brought forward from angels to help heal and harmonize.

Aura
A distinctive atmosphere surrounding a person or thing. A luminous radiation which emanates from all living matters. An energy field that interpenetrates with and radiates out beyond the physical and which is made up of different vibrations or frequencies. Also referred to as our subtle energy field or our electromagnetic energy field.

Chakra
A Sanskrit word meaning "wheel." One of the energy centers within the body. The main function of a chakra is to act as a transformer for the higher frequency subtle energies of the aura.

Chi
The nutritive subtle energy taken in during breathing. Also referred to as prana or ki.

Clairvoyance
The ability to see the aura with its colours, thought forms, shapes, etc. Clairvoyant abilities are mediated through the use of the brow chakra.

Holistic
A synergistic approach that deals with the whole of a human (physical, mental, emotional and spiritual aspects) to maintain optimum health.

Karma
Chosen learning process, effect.

Kundalini
The awakening or sleeping "serpent power." Located in the root chakra. Energy for spiritual growth. The flowering of all seven chakras awakens the Kundalini, bringing cosmic consciousness. The power that rises from the base chakra to the crown.

Mantra
Words of Power. A sounded meditation used for manifestation.

Meridian
The highest point or stage of development. Body energy flows in specific pathways, which is referred to as meridians.

Manipura
City of Jewels or Lustrous Gem. The chakra located over the navel under the chest. Also known as the solar plexus chakra.

Mudladhara
Root or Support. The chakra located at the end of the spine referred to as the root or base chakra.

Sanskrit
An ancient Indic language that is the language of Hinduism and the Vedas and the classical literary language of India.

Sahasrara
Thousandfold. The chakra localized on the top of your head also referred to as the crown chakra.

Svadhisthana
Sweetness or One's Own Abode. The chakra-hara chakra. Also referred to as the spleen or navel chakra.

Vishuddha
Purity. The chakra located in the throat and referred to as the throat chakra.

Subtle Energy
A general term that denotes energy that exists outside our physical reality.

Super consciousness
One's higher consciousness.

Vibration
Refers to subtle or electromagnetic energy in varying frequencies and amplitudes.

Index

A

abundance 11, 32
addictive traits 12
adrenals 43
Amber 38, 39, 96, 99
Amethyst 96, 99
anxiety 18, 32
Aventurine 32, 33, 96, 99

B

balance 39, 43, 71, 96, 99
Balance 93
beliefs 24, 91
Blue ... 24, 25, 26, 27, 91, 96, 99

C

calming essence 18
candle 13, 19, 25, 31, 38, 44, 50, 75, 85
Celestine 19, 20, 96, 99
circulatory system 50
Citrine 38, 39, 96, 99

clairvoyance 19
clarity 1, 18, 20, 25, 43
communication 5, 27, 82
Communication .. 38, 96, 97, 99
confidence 25, 93
confused 5, 25, 49, 60
confusion 4, 18, 32, 83
connectedness 12
courage 50
creative 24, 37, 38, 43
Crown ... 4, 9, 11, 12, 13, 14, 89, 96, 97, 99
Crown Chakra 12

D

depression 5, 43, 95, 99
Devotion 96, 99
dismayed 49

E

emotional 32, 69, 101
energy 5, 8, 9, 11, 14, 18, 19, 20, 21, 24, 25, 27, 32, 34, 39, 43, 44, 45, 49, 50, 52,

53, 56, 59, 60, 61, 78, 83, 99, 100, 101, 102, 103
enthusiasm..........................43
esophagus...........................25

F

fears............................ 12, 24
feeling down 12
focus...18, 25, 43, 45, 49, 50, 52, 53
Focus 53, 96, 99
friends 2, 31, 33, 58, 92
fulfillment...........................43

G

Gabrial 46, 96
Green .31, 32, 33, 34, 92, 96, 99
grief 43
grounded............................49
Grounding..........................96

H

Harmony.............................96
headaches..........................32
healer 31, 32
health 31, 77, 101

Heart....4, 31, 33, 34, 92, 96, 97, 99
Hematite 50, 96, 99
higher self 9, 11, 34, 38
higher understanding........37
hormones...........................43

I

ideals 24
imagination........................12
immune functions..............12
Indigo........ 18, 19, 20, 96, 99
inner strength 43, 71, 72
Insomnia.............................19
Inspiration 96, 99
intuition...................... 19, 90

J

Jophiel....3, 4, 37, 38, 39, 40, 41, 42, 78, 96
joy..11

L

Labradorite 25, 26, 96, 99
larynx 25
legs 50
liver 38

love 1, 2, 3, 5, 7, 9, 11, 12, 21, 28, 33, 34, 40, 46, 53, 61, 64, 68, 69, 70, 72, 73, 77, 78, 79, 81, 82, 83, 84, 85, 92
lower back 50, 95

M

Meditation.......................... 19
Mental awareness 38
Michael 3, 24, 25, 27, 28, 29, 30, 70, 75, 96
miracles 31

N

new career 49

O

Orange 39, 43, 44, 45, 94, 96, 99
Orange Calcite 44, 96, 99
overzealous 49

P

pain 5, 19, 27, 32, 77, 82, 92, 94, 95

pain tolerance 32
pancreas............................. 38
pineal gland....................... 12
positive 7, 43, 68, 99
Power.......................... 97, 101
psychic 19, 90, 99

R

Raphael ... 3, 4, 1, 31, 32, 33, 34, 35, 36, 83, 96
Raziel ... 3, 18, 19, 20, 21, 22, 23, 96
Red 50, 51, 95, 96, 99
resiliency............................ 50
Root. 4, 9, 49, 50, 52, 95, 96, 97, 99, 102

S

Sacral ... 4, 43, 44, 45, 94, 96, 97, 99
sad 25
security 50, 95
self doubt............... 11, 37, 99
Self respect 43
shy...................................... 25
Solar Plexus 4, 37, 38, 39, 93, 96, 97, 99
speaking....................... 24, 25

speech 24, 25
Spiritually............................38
spleen 38, 102
stability................................50
stomach..................... 38, 93

T

Third Eye ... 4, 18, 19, 20, 90, 96, 97, 99
Throat .. 4, 24, 27, 91, 96, 97, 99
thyroid 25
tired.....................................49
toxins........................... 34, 38
traumas 50
truth 1, 11, 14, 21, 24, 32, 40, 53, 77, 82, 83, 84, 85

U

untruths 12
Uriel 3, 4, 49, 50, 52, 53, 54, 55, 70, 82, 83, 96

V

Violet ..11, 13, 14, 89, 96, 99
Violet Ray 11, 13, 14

W

wisdom..... 1, 2, 4, 18, 20, 37, 71, 72, 99
Wisdom 19, 96
writers 37
writing............. 13, 24, 50, 75

Y

Yellow .37, 38, 39, 93, 96, 99

Z

Zadkiel .3, 11, 12, 13, 14, 15, 16, 17, 96

Sources

∞

Chakra Company allowed the use of charts and chakra information. Thank you Suzanne for your generosity and expertise!

Visit their site at: http://www.chakracompany.com.

Thank you again to Rassouli for the beautiful art.
Visit his gallery at: http://www.rassouli.com/

The chakra images are from Wikipedia Commons which is a freely licensed media file repository. The original owner of the images has a great site for chakra related information and training. Go to http://www.sacredcenters.com for more details

Made in the USA
Charleston, SC
24 February 2010